Ruminative Words

Fritzinie Lavoile

Ruminative Words

CONTENTS

I.   Onward to My Faithful Journey to the sun   Pg #1

II.   Into the Breaking   Pg #17

III.   Wounded Soul   Pg #31

IV.   Escape   Pg #51

V.   Into the Making   Pg #81

VI.   Caught like a Feather in a Jar I am no Longer Floating   Pg #103

VII.   Final Form   Pg #133

Chapter I:

Onward to My Faithful Journey to the Sun

May our love be like the branches on a tree...
which not even the strongest of winds could break.
May our love rise above obstacles...
that block its path towards the light.
May our love stretch its every inch
as it reaches for life.

Let our love be as timeless as decades
flowing seamlessly into seconds.
Let it be one whose interest never wavers...
only fights to grow stronger.
Let our love strive to stay attached
against the pull of the harsh world.

When the days are dark,
when the storm threatens to tear us apart,
love me as the sun loves the tree.
Healing it. Caressing it. Helping it thrive to its fullest.

Love me like the leaves on the tree
adapting to seasonal challenges.
Shedding our insecurities. Our doubts. Our mistakes.
Letting them go along with the cold.
A few might turn dull and fall off
But will always gracefully blossom better than the last.

A love that carries such great energy.
Brimming beauty...
Attracting all of life.

You might say this is cliché.
But trust me when I say
these feelings shall simply not decay.

Our love will always be alive in my thoughts.
Random sounds of your laughter still echo through my
ears.
Random flashes of your smile still project through my
eyes.

My mind is full of our memories.
A flash drive stuck in its port.
No matter how hard I try to pull away
it simply does not budge.

When the night comes, I think of you.
Just as I've done every day since we met.
It seems it's wrong to love you.
The world has been against us since day one.

You and I are meant to be.
But the world is cruel,
and our families are fools,
for keeping us apart.
When it's clear the moon shines just to make way for us.

I know even if our bodies are miles apart
our minds are connected by the single thought of us.

I would pause the world
if I had the power.
To spend one more night with you.
To feel your warmth on me,
the tingle of your breath on me.

My nights will never be complete without you.
Because I can't go on having you only in my dreams
and encountering our memories only through our songs.

Why can't we escape this place?
Why can't we move away
from those who desire to tear us apart?
Why can't we travel to a land that's far
Instead of wishing for each other through the stars?

I wish we owned every night
that will come for the rest of our lives.
I wish we could inscribe upon them
the beautiful letters of our last names.
But we don't.

At least not in this lifetime.

I cannot remember if I saw you or you saw me first.
All that I remember is the moment we finally spoke
with more than just eye contact across the room.

The breeze blows your scent to me.
Every time I get pulled closer.
Our eyes speak with a depth reminiscent of the spiritual.
Plunging us deep into one another's soul.
I yearn for your kiss,
waiting for your hand at my side.
At that moment I understand that
you are meant to be mine.

I lay my head on your chest
and I hear your heartbeat echo through your shirt.
My mind wonders what your lips will taste like.
I reimagine the plumpness against mine.

When I do,
my lips receive the flutters of a butterfly kiss.
It is the sweetest sensation that I cannot resist.
Kissing you is like drinking the purest of waters
from streams only found in heaven.

-Loving through the Senses

From the moment I hear your voice…
nothing but smiles.

From the moment I feel your touch…
everything …
everything and an addition of butterflies.

I wish the world looked at you the way I do
Then they would see
How precious you are
How caring
How delicate
How safe

I close my eyes,
my attempt to dream of you.
For it is the only way I am able to keep you close.
I reminisce on our beautiful moments
and every image conjured is a simple source of joy.
My heart feels as though you are the only piece meant to fit.
A hole perfectly created for you.

-space

If ever I were to get lost in space
I would not be upset.
I am in the same place where our memories live.
A space that carries every echo of our voice.
Where the farther I drift, the further back I can go
to relive our history,
watch over our story,
and take notes of all the mistakes I made.
So that whenever I drift back to Earth
I would know how to trace the exact steps
that led me to you.

Do not ask me to love you halfway,
as that would be asking a race car to drive slowly.
For I tend to overflow with passion.
I will attack with full force.
I cannot fathom how to love you without being obsessed.
I cannot comprehend how I would hold you without the
sole purpose of feeling every inch of you.
I cannot imagine how I would kiss you without the purpose
being to consume you.
I want to hear you. I want to touch you. I want to feel you.
I cannot choose the percentage of affection to give.
Its either all of me or none.

Teach me how to love you patiently.
To be comfortable without your presence.
Not to feel like there is a part of me missing.

Help me to accept how we can grow apart
and our connection can still be powerful.
How physical touch does not equate emotional
involvement.
Give me the reassurance that missing you,
is not losing you.

Our love does not have to be all consuming to be real.

Chapter II:
Into the Breaking

Stranger,
keeper of all my secrets.
I never thought you could do this to me
and so easily too.

How quick you were to forget.
The one who said I love you
but to only use me.

I never should have accepted you
under that starry night.
Should have stuck to your first goodbye.
Never imagined you would break my heart
a second time.

I never should have helped.
I never should have carried your pain as my own.
I never should have held you while you cried.

When I looked into your eyes that first time,
what I saw then was a soul who needed a mate.
But I should have known it should have never been me.

Now a stranger is all I can see.

I can't say I didn't see it coming.
Your eyes spoke volumes.

Softly but surely
they were telling me things
that my ears didn't want to pay attention to.

Going through the emotions.
Obsessed with your devotion.
Realizing you wanted me more than I wanted myself.

I let you come and go as you wish.
You animated me like a puppet
even with no strings.

I said I loved you,
then I said I hated you.
I'm angry.
I want to replace you.

But I can't help myself.
For if ever you're gone
I may lose my mind.

You got me going through numerous emotions
when I do the simplest actions.
I still find myself flipping through our memories
like it is a true obsession.

I sometimes think I'm over you
but then you come back around
and you flip my emotions upside down.

You should have come with a warning.
One that would have loudly proclaimed:

"Observe me from afar
just the way an explosion pulls you in with all its colors
do not attempt to get too close

just stroll past me

I will not blame you for not stopping
because I am a bomb waiting to explode
and I am determined to destroy everything in my vicinity."

We are two cracked souls
patiently counting the days until they shatter.

It's our subconscious pulling us close,
stacking all our bombs together
in hopes of creating a greater explosion.

The kind where shards of us continue to fall
long after we are gone.

I was once told that I destroy everything I touch
and for a while that became my reality.

I would find the most beautiful leaves
and tear them apart.

I would build a sandcastle
with no intention of letting it stand.

We were fated to stay together
but only in poetry.

Every letter seemingly made for each other.
Every sentence in the perfect order.
In a way we were always poetry.

Only our actions held double entendre
and it was only later I started to recognize it.

We were going in opposite directions.
I needed to fly,
but you wanted to stay grounded.
Even then I was confident
we were headed in the right direction.
We didn't kiss goodbye.
We never kissed again.
But we remain in poetry.

It is where the beauty of our worlds
can be rearranged into what I hoped we would be.

It scares me how much I give of myself involuntarily.
How much I trust that people are genuine.
How much I trust that it's safe to close my eyes.
How much I trust that this building won't fall,
that the ground won't cave in.

It's all too much....

I imagined that this time when I blew you away
you would be like the leaves
coming again the next year
to grow back right where I left you.

What seemed to me like diamonds
were only droplets of water
reflecting light from the sun

It's funny how we told ourselves that there will always be
sparks each time we kissed.
It's funny too how each time we were wrong.

If you looked closely at my heart
you would still find the fingerprints
from when your hands held on so tight.

You rejected my body
but still you wanted my heart.

If ever you run into the girl I used to be...

promise me you would whisper these secrets to her:

>Don't trust the first smile someone gives you.
>Trust the first time they yell at you.
>Walk away from anything that disrupts your peace of mind.
>Please value your peace of mind.

Spare her too a little bit of kindness
because she is stumbling around to find me.
Please take her home to me
because she's broken,
and sees herself as flawed.

No one exists to save her
from the monsters in her nightmares.
The only thing I can do is
heighten the feelings in her gut.
But she doesn't know that they are warnings
she mistakes them for nervous butterflies.

Chapter III:
Wounded Soul

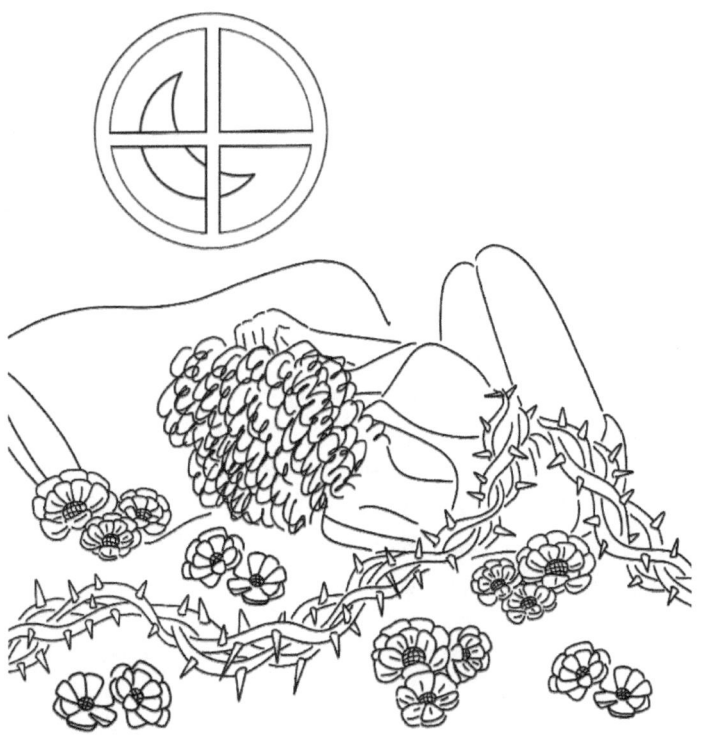

-My Spirit Out in the Open Like Roadkill

Cold wind strikes my skin.
Each gust hits me like
sharp shards of glass.
It attacks every inch of me.
Cuts down to the bone
and deep into my core.
I fall numb to the pain
as shivers turn me warm.
I take comfort in the affliction
my fear slowly transitions into love.
It's compulsive. It's all consuming.
Bruises or leftover kisses.
I can no longer tell the difference.
My soul tied to yours for eternity.
You are all that I want to see
even if you're the one blinding me.
Your voice is all that I desire.
The screeching torture bleeds my ears.
Your air is all I crave
full of toxins poisoning me.
I will breathe you in until I die.
I won't ever leave.
I won't even try.

I will love you to my grave and back.

-How To Bury a Heart

I have figured out how to not care.
Take every word said to you at face value.
Never let your thoughts run deep
so you won't find deeper meanings where they do not exist.

Because once the roots start to plant
you won't be cruel enough to pluck the flowers.
Start by never spilling out your waters.
Save up your fire.
Use it to light the candle within yourself.
Seal in the warmth.
So your heart may never experience the pain of being
frozen and shattered.

I was loving you unconditionally.
Every time you comforted me.
Every time you blew my mind.
Every time you made me feel beautiful.
Every time your lips touched mine.
Every time our eyes met, and I could not stop smiling.

For what we shared was wonderful.
Not a moment had me feeling wasteful.
For every second that I was with you
I was faithful.

Everyone else left so why wouldn't you?
You say you won't leave.
But deep down even I know your words are not true.
Yet...you still made me believe in you.
There was no reason for you to stay.
I saw it fading from your eyes.
All the love...I watched as the bright sparkles
fizzled into dull grays.
I thought with more time
you would once again become mine.
But that too was fantasy.
That too was a wish made up from insanity.

-The Boundless Energy of Soul Ties.

I find it puzzling how the union of two beautiful souls
can fast transform into shackles.
Ever since I let you in
my body no longer houses just me.

My door has become unhinged
loudly screeching the voices of other inhabitants.
Ever since I shook your hand
and I agreed to be your friend...
I have felt the weight of you pulling me down
as the negativity propels the drown of my spirit.

My body: Deteriorating.
My mind: Infuriated.

My mind is home to feelings that are not mine.
I am trapped on an island filled with your ghosts.
I am a sponge absorbing all your thoughts.
I have feet cemented to the ground
there is no letting go.
Other personalities are talking.
In strange feet I see myself walking.

I was a holy garden
that let poison plant its roots.

I want you to be gone.
I want to start to heal
but not completely.
Because you see…

I want to cherish the feelings that came with your presence.
Chills running down my spine.
Cheeks hurting from the smiles.
A stomach filled with the loveliest butterflies.
Happiness that makes me want to dance even in the sky.

I do not want the ones that came after.
Eyes full of tears.
Head close to exploding.
Vision going blind.
Pain in my stomach.
 Uncontrollable shaking.
   Heart
        stopped
              beating.

I hold my breath
and clutch my chest.
Every time my heart beats
the rhythm that our souls
no longer dance to.

It hurts so much when I reminisce
I lose my thoughts of what it was like
before you.

After you there existed rhythm but no dancing

I remember finding out about your deception.
And oh…how I wanted to get you out of my system.

I could not believe how the one I thought I loved
had transformed into a stranger all at once.

-    A note to the rain

Let me cry with you.
Watch you pour down so hard.
Let out your anger. Rage. sadness.

Let me hear you thunder
see your lightning strike.
Observe your strength in its full expression.
All of it is beautifully inspiring.

So let me cry with you.
Let me dwell in our mixed emotions.
Because then I would not be doing it alone.

Let me feed off your strength.
Till I can cry alone.
Maybe until I am strong enough not to cry at all.

My heart is racing
Heavy breathing
Eyes are tearing
My body is shaking
My mind is an earthquake
I can feel the volcano rubbing on the inside
My blood is flowing like melted lava
My skin is hotter than coal
My thoughts are out of my control
No mercy in my eyes
I want destruction
I hold no thoughts of peace in my mind.

What was once as smooth as an ocean's surface
turned suddenly turbulent.
Roughened by the typhoon winds of your actions.
The damage will certainly be permanent.
Treason is never truly expected
it can only be served by the hands fully trusted.
At a loss for words. At a loss of nerves.

Under the impression ships were imperishable.
Slapped by the realization
that nothing was truly indestructible.
Shipwrecked on this journey, cast away from me are
all the secrets that I thought we never had.
I soon figured out what you were trying to hide.
The fog cleared away
Now I am able to see
the warnings were about you
the stormy sea.

The beautiful skin that I sacrificed
was once again not worth it.
Or maybe
it was the short-lived happiness which justified it.
Every scar was a beautiful reminder
of the puzzle pieces we drew in together.
Again, and again until there were no
clearer spots left to scar.

Until I felt fully engulfed in your love.

I have rivers running down my face.
Racing each other to see who will be the first.
Racing to watch who shall take the lead and
fill the hole I made in the dirt.

Feeling trapped
torn in two.

Wanting to scream
but not wanting to be heard too.

How did you stab me in the back
only to turn around and lie to the world
that you were the one bleeding?

My excitement slowly began to fade as
I began to sink onto the floor
clutching my stomach with one hand
and the other on my face.

The moon's light reflected off my dress.
It was as though my dismay were a spectacle
in need of spotlight.
It was as though it needed an audience cheering:
"And there goes another one!!!"
with not a hint of shock in their voice.

I let the cold breeze consume all of me.
My body shivered in the cold
and I slipped off my heels,
letting the wet grass numb my toes.
For this was the irony of nature's beauty.
As I started the journey back home,
my feelings seemed connected to the weather
because the sky started pouring out all what I felt inside.

Sounds of lightning blasted by my ears.
one-drop-at-a-time
tears streamed from my eyes
mixing with the rain
running past my face.

I unzipped myself till I was bare and in my natural state.
I let the water run down every inch of me and take with it
all the desperation I could muster.
I looked up at the sky and screamed until my tonsils ached
until I was spitting blood…

With nothing on me,
with no weight pulling me down
I opened my door.
My home took me as I was.
Naked. Bleeding. In pain.

I sat in front of my mirror
picking out the grass from my wounds
gazing endlessly at my wounded soul.
Even though I knew it would be a while
before I walked without pain,
I knew still that I would cherish every moment ahead.

Chapter IV:
Escape

It was through living in a fantasy
that I found the means to escape my reality.
It was by running away into someone else's home
that I found the means to escape my reality.
It was through seeking love in someone else's arms
that I found the means to escape my reality.

-Let us Go Back to Life Before

If I could start my life over…
letting go of everything.
Fall back into my mother's womb.
Retrace my steps to undo the damage done to my heart.

If I could start my life over…
go back and avoid the unnecessary struggle,
unnecessary people.
Retrace every step.
Retake every test.
Take back what I have spoken.
Undo all my actions.

If I could start my life over…
back into my mother's arms.
Back into her womb.
Into the protective abyss
away from all the damage.

I would hold tight,
afraid to step into the fire
of this freighting world.

I would keep my eyes shut.

In need of a substance.
An essence to fill the void.
A presence to feel secure.
Not that it matters what it is.
 As long as it is there…
    the drugs,
      the alcohol,
    my rain,
the pain…
Reality would fade.
Maybe even for a second.
Overlooking the
    mistreatment,
      the neglect,
    the abuse
Just for that presence.
 Afraid of its absence…
      loneliness would drown me back down.
   Force me to accept whatever is thrown
from blind sentiment.
Creating the immense delusion
of completion.
Of feeble satisfaction.

We are all addicted to something that can ruin us.
Temporary pleasures that still cannot make us whole.

One more bite
One more sip
One more pull
One more trip
One more kiss
One more time
Just one last time
We often say to ourselves every time…

-    Imagine Free Falling Way Up from Space

Rising beyond your sky
against the strength of your pull.
Leaving a world beneath me.
One I once lived in,
so big but now invisible.

I wonder how the clouds would feel
when I let go,
when I fall back into the atmosphere.
When I give in to gravity.

Would it give me the comfort I am longing for?
Soften my nerves?
Cool off my burns?

No doubt in my mind.
No fear in my heart.
Just a yearning to be set free.
To feel alive.

And maybe that starts with dying.
Maybe that starts with letting
the earth shatters me to pieces.
Maybe that simply starts with
letting go of the fear of new beginnings.

When our tongues cannot hold the weight of our thoughts,
when they are never enough
to express all the emotions we carry,
how then do we explain what we find to be unexplainable?

When centuries of dialect refuse to collide
refuse to relieve the pressure boiling inside.
How do we give life to the
yet unformed laying on our tongues?

No matter what we say.
No matter how we say it.
No matter what language.
No matter how many times.
The words will never reflect
what is truly inside.

Running through the resistance
no matter the distance
all tribulations are numbed.
For a moment I am freed
amongst all the chaos I can finally breathe.
My mind is cleared
for a moment I can disappear.
In control of my journey
there is no mystery
no uncertainty.
So yes,
running through the storm
that is where I find my calm.
No tears. No stress.

Just infinite progress...

Today I did something.
I spent the day in bed.
I'm not sure why,
I was telling my body to get up
but it wasn't listening.
I was telling it that I don't want to
waste so much of my time.
I've already wasted so much time...doing nothing.
But it laid there as if it was trapped under a ton.
I did not have the will power to force my body up today.
So...I let it take over.
And eventually it gave some power back to me.
Just enough to force myself into the shower.
Just enough to put the spoon to my mouth
and get back under the covers.

I no longer have a sense of time.
I wake up and the day seems to have already gone by...

There is a cave deep inside my head.

It is where I run to
and put together
all the collected pieces
of my broken self.

-In Need of a Rescue

Sometimes I feel like I am still that six-year-old girl in Haiti.
In the middle of an earthquake.
Stuck under that brick wall.
Everyone trampling on top of me
yearning to survive,
deafened to my cries.

I am constantly reminded
that the last time something like this
was forced onto me
it crushed me.
And I needed someone's else's saving.
Every time I let someone close, they betray me.
Every time I think we are both falling
its only my own heart that breaks.

Theirs remains whole
because they never truly shared it with me.

I wish you and I could be close.
I wish you and I had a bond which could never come loose.
You are the only one I have
but it feels like you're not even there.
All the yelling. All the insults.
Makes me wish that I was elsewhere.

- My Toxic Trait Is Being Blind by Default

"What was the greatest trick of the devil? Convincing the world that it did not exist."
-Charles Baudelaire

It was so subtle
an ingenious plan in his mind.
Gaining the trust of the world
walking amongst us in disguise.
Fooling us into feeling safe.
Allowing us to think everything was good
and that nothing was at stake.
Greeting us with a beguiling smile in the light
while stabbing us sadistically in the back at night.
Bringing about ugly scars that we could not see.
Wondering why everyone we met ran away.
Begging: *"Please tell me, what is wrong with me?"*
Making us believe it was our fault.
The destruction and the lies.
Telling us we were not worth it
daring us to take our lives.
But our eyes were opened
by the All Mighty and Divine.
You my friend are the devil
and I am no longer blind.

- The teachings of a budding mind

Which am I supposed to believe?
When you tell me I'm beautiful when you are happy?
Or when you call me worthless when you are angry?
That you love me, and I make you proud?
Or that I'm a disappointment and you are ashamed?
Make up your mind
to help me make up mine.
Don't beat me up more than I already do.
It's not helping me mentally.
Now even if it's not from you
when I hear the word beautiful
I know worthlessness will follow.

Don't hide me from the sun and its beauty
and expect me to still thrive.

Water my roots with kind words
so that I grow confident.
Not bent out of shape by insecurities.
Not stunted in growth
all because you were drenching me in vinegar.

\-   Escape Plan

I know when someone is mad at me
all I have to do is tell them what they want to hear.
Stay silent and take the insult.
Don't voice my opinion
because *"that's disrespectful"* ...
Let them take their anger out on me
they will eventually calm down.
After all, the anger is coming from a place of love.

It's your fault they got angry.
Do better.
Just smile.
Act like everything is fine.
You can't provide for yourself yet
just wait until it's your time.

"Don't ever let a man put his hands on you"
as you do just that.

"Don't ever let a man insult you"
as you do just that.

"It was all out of love"
I hear you say.

He also tells me that.

When we finally encounter ourselves
we ask *how could I have accepted this for so long*?
And then we look back at our parents.
Those we called friends.
Those who we spent most of our days looking up to.
I'm speaking of our teachers.
And then we wonder *how we accepted this for so long?*
How could we learn to respect ourselves
if our examples did not respect us?
Was there ever a time when
Black people were treated with respect?
Was there ever a time
when my elders treated *me* with respect?
So how could I have known respect
enough to treat it to myself?

When raised by unhappy people
it is difficult to not also become unhappy yourself.
When raised with violence
it almost becomes second nature
to seek violence out yourself.

Unstable homes do not always look like those with drugs
no.
An unstable home may just look like
a hard working "responsible" family.

They say that our brains often make up details to fill in the gap.
They say that it can just entirely block out the trauma.
I cannot remember much of my childhood
But still…there's that one experience that plays like a tape loop in my head.
Sometimes I imagine that no matter how old I grow
the details will always remain threaded in my mind's fabric.

There are some things we simply will not fully understand
until years later.
There are some actions you do not know were wrong until
time elapses into newer years.

Before then it often looked right to you.
Look at all of history…
every person we have come to regard as a villain today
all thought they were doing the right thing.
Just like them
I too thought that my mistakes were the right thing.

They can't be the only ones to bear the blame, right?
I have a brain... too.
I have a mouth... too.
I could have screamed... too.
I could have run... too.

I chose to stay regardless.
Did my staying mean that I wanted it... too?

Only years later
will you understand that what you thought was okay
was not at all okay.

only years later
will that realization sink in.

Sometimes you just wished you had screamed a little louder
picked up your legs and ran.

Maybe told someone. Maybe told anyone.

Only years later.

Why do I remember the act
and still not remember their faces or their names?

That is honestly the truth.
I feel like a haunted house.
I feel as though numerous ghosts feel happy
spooking my dreams occasionally.

I never asked you to
yet you filled up all the holes in my body.
I never said yes to you
yet you continued to pour
until there was no room left for joy.

When your mess overflowed onto the floor
you told me to throw on a smile
you told me to clean it up with pride.
You told me that my body was mine
and I was the one responsible for what happened to it.

Today, I yell back at you.
You never asked me if I wanted to!
I never said yes to you!
How could I answer when I was being choked?
When your friends were laughing through every stroke.

Through it all...
I could only smell your sweat mixing with my blood.
I could only sense the silent nods behind the cameras.

Boys will be boys they say.
But why did I have to be your toy?

I am the survivor of three crimes tonight.
Theft, rape, and murder.
All because you could not control
your urge to see me naked.
Even underneath all my baggy clothes
I was still not protected.

So, when I get told that it's "*not all men*"
I am transported back to the faces behind the cameras
to the men who chose to ignore.

Why is it that the threat of attack from an invisible boyfriend is more frightening compared to the pleading words of a visible woman?

Everyone pontificates about why one must be self-aware.
But no one readily answers the question: "How do you
discover yourself?"
So, I will.
You discover yourself through your mistakes
For it is through trying and failing
that you come to realize three guiding lessons:

> what you want to continue to do.
> what you want to never do again.
> who you want to never meet again.

I have stopped letting myself feel comfortable
in arms that embrace yet speak only of empty promises.

Chapter V:
Into the Making

-    Snowflakes Are Made from Angel Dust

Like a fingerprint, each is uniquely made.
Specially crafted, there are no two alike.
Much like you and I, attentively hand designed.
Drifting down from the Heavens to Earth.
Time slows to capture the beauty and worth.
The innocent joy that was once brought.
Now ruined by all these tainted thoughts.
The sight of you now is so rare.
I wonder how you'd feel on my skin bare.
Too precious for my sinful hands.
Melting as you quietly land.

- The City

One by one up the stairs into the city where the dead walk
among us:
the ones whose dreams died before they could be born.
The ones who hit a stunt in their growth and never
recovered.

One by one down the road into the city full of people
determined to be the next big thing.
Distracted from the stench of sadness the sidewalks bare.

One by one I must warn them
that this is the place where
Hell hides in the shadows
preying on the young and alive
waiting to devour the hope
in their eyes.

One by one this city will eat you alive.

Ruminative Words

I am made of two shades of life.
Obsessed with the coldness of rain
yet still yearning for warmth from sunlight.
Taught to camouflage the ugly
and amplify the beauty.
Block out the dark
and embrace the light.

Even my iris and skin are confused
on the proper shades to show,
the percentage of brown to glow.

Then you came around
and started mixing your colors on my canvas.
No longer bland I found it beautiful.
Until I realized you were painting a picture of you.
Erasing my beauty marks and drawing only scars.
I almost forgot how colorful I once was.

Sharpening my brushstrokes trying closely to resemble
myself again.
...But able to recognize pieces of you in the background.

I am made of two shades of life.
Still learning how to blend into even tones.
I didn't get to choose all my colors
but I will use them to paint a masterpiece.
Highlighting the depths of all the Hues in my heart,
because everything named priceless is a collection of
emotional strokes and shades.

-    Sincerely, a Haitian Girl in America

What a mental shift…
From wondering if I was going to eat, to if I looked neat,
well put together, worth the racial slur.

Back in my country…
Back in Beautiful Haiti
we all looked the same.
Race wasn't a thing there. At least it was not to me.

It wasn't until I hopped on that JetBlue plane
that I saw a white face that wasn't on a screen.
It wasn't until I was accused of being too dark
that I began wishing for a different kind of skin.
It wasn't until I was in a classroom
surrounded by silky straight hair
that I cried because mine wasn't complying.

When I hopped on that plane my life completely changed.
I cannot say it was all for better
because of course some parts are worse.
But I find it funny
how we are all on earth
Made up from dirt.
In the middle of the grand infinite magic called the
universe.
Surrounded by even more space.
But here I am having to worry about my race.

- Being Black is My Superpower

See my color
and see my struggle.
Do not be blind to my troubles.
See my hair
and learn the roots from which they grew.
See my breast
and prize the milk that flows through.
See my body
and foster the seeds that it carries.
See my eyes
and engrave the waters that they bury.
See my skin
and the sun beaming off me.
See my color
and know my fury.
See my color
and make an effort to understand.
My exhaustion. My raging pains.
Eliminate the perpetual hate.
See my color
and simply love me for it.

Here does not feel like home
I've never fit in.
Not even if I've wanted to
Not even when I've tried to.

I make the effort to see the world from their perspective
but they were not born
staring into the same light that I did.
Hearing the same screams that I did.
Seeing the same violence that I did.
Feeling the same pain that I did.

-      When you hear those sirens singing…

Hold your breath
you'll be in for quite a swim.
It is wise not to resist.
Just give in.
Don't run.
You won't win.
Fall into their harmony.
Hopefully they're not having a bad day.
Put your hands up.
Get ready for the dive.
There's a chance you won't come back up.
Drift slowly to the sound.
Let the sirens pin you down.
Give them control of your body.
Pray to God to forgive your sins.
Your fate is in His hands.
Maybe it'll be a smooth ride.
Maybe you'll make it back to shore.
Maybe you'll get to appreciate the sound
of another night's snore.

Yes,
trauma too gets passed down genetically
just light brown eyes
just like curly hair
just like plump lips
just like white praise…

You already assumed the worst
and so I went out and simply did the worst.

Why do you seem so shocked
when your wishes came true?

I fought so hard to be seen as white through your eyes
but when a person's eyes
are glazed by years of dirt filled hate
of course I would be seen as though I was dirty.
So I too became that

blame yourself not me.

Different thoughts
Different views
Different skin
Different rules

\-   Love Letter to My Melanin

Soft to the touch
Warmth in the cold
Coolness in the heat
Strength when I am weak
Foundation in life
There through all the seasons
Comfort through all my emotions
Always there
You always were
Absorbing every tear
Healing every scar
You are the essence of my being
The color to my skin
You are beautiful
Even when I was hating you
You were loving me harder.

Caged by society
buried under the deity
women were not allowed to dress comfortably.
Skirts below the ankles
sleeves long past the elbows.
To this day the slightest reveal of the shoulders
and the entire world flips over.
Your bra straps cannot show
but don't you dare think of not wearing one.
Because my dear sisters *"you must hide away your nipples."*
Yes, you must hide away the same ones
made to give sustenance to the entire human race.
Those are unacceptable especially when it's feeding a life.
Unless of course it is dressed up and put on a show
for them to throw their bills.
Or used like a plate to catch their spills.
Even that has a time they must once again be put away.
Because they are now saggy
no longer good for entertainment
no longer shaped like a perfect cup.
You must choose to either
be prized for your body
but have your personality overlooked
or show off your intelligence
but for that you must have vigilance.

Over sexualized for doing the least of sexual things.
Being mature does not always come with age.
Not when older men regularly approach young girls.
Or older women: young boys.

Expected not to say a thing
because of course no one would believe them.
Not when they haven't even gotten their periods.
Or have yet to grow a strand of pubic hair.
Because surely, what would a fine man find himself
attracted to?

But I bet the children are wondering that too.
So the only option is for them to stay silent.
Because you're supposed to enjoy
having the power to turn heads.
Even if it's not the ones you yourself are attracted to.

You tell me I am too young to have a boyfriend.
But am I not also too young for these men?
But I wasn't warned about that.
Because apparently there's an age limit.
And until then you can't know about anything sexual.
Because you believe everyone will respect me,
no one will touch me in the places
that they are not supposed to.
Because my innocence matters and it should be treasured.
Because I will never experience being violated by anyone.

Allow me to shed light upon your oblivion.
Do not bash me for being sexual
without asking me if any of it was consensual.
Explain to me the dangers of predators
and encourage me to believe that my words matter.
Update your parenting methods:
Because the world is fast downgrading.
Don't be oblivious and think we're still in the old times.
Not when I'm experiencing the real world
at this time while you remain in your pretentious bubble.

One that leaves you convinced
that blinding me was protecting me from the world.
Not when the world's prime mission is to destroy me.
Not when tearing someone's innocence is celebrated.
Not when evading the same box that is called so precious
is not met with any repercussions.

That same box that I'm supposed to hide from the world.
That same box that I'm supposed to keep under locks and
keys until a man comes along with the perfect ring.

I no longer live in a fairytale, and neither should you.

- Buried Innocence

Where did she go?
The girl with the smile whose length could run for miles.
How deep did she go?
How many layers of myself
would I have to peel to feel her skin?

The girl who looked at life with soft eyes.
Eyes not yet roughened from reality.
The girl who could still believe
in the fantasy of a happy life.

I've heard so much about her.
How she loved to dance and sing.
How she was not at all shy to the world.

One day I'll muster the courage to introduce myself
to the stranger that lives inside of me.
But it's been so long
and I fear that she has already turned to stone.
One day I'll remember enough about her
to write a proper eulogy.
I would bring vibrant flowers
that reflected her personality
with a letter of apology.
One saying I am sorry for allowing myself to forget her and
not giving the world a proper chance to meet her.

Is it not strange how with some people we actually get along better
.... but only from a distance?

Do not ask me why I'm not responding.
It is because the conversations are in my head.
Because I like the responses that I give to myself.
Because I would rather hear your story instead.

Do not ask me to lift my voice so that you could hear.
Because I think that might just make me tear.
Because you don't understand how hard it is.
Because even I don't understand why that is.

But I will speak if it means I'll lift up your frown.
Yell out for help so that you may not drown.

But I think I'm getting better because speaking is not as
exhausting as it used to be.
Because you make me want to speak
as much as I want to stay silent.
Because to speak is to now set my soul free.

I do not know what is worse:

The awareness of a world immersed in suffering.
                        Or
The awareness of my miniscule role in freeing it.

The last few days were so long.

I did not know yet what was to come
but I could feel it.
The brightness of the world shined a little brighter.
It was as though nature had a premonition of my departure.

So the flowers stood taller;
bloomed louder.
The wind blew warmer
and rain seemed to disappear.
The sun lasted a little longer
trying to convince me the days had more to uncover
trying to convince me to stay.

I found a home made out of cardboard on the subway
and kissed the park floor good night.
I listened to the late night playing of the street bands.
The sounds softly faded away as I travelled
further and further into my dreams.
You see:
My dreams are the only place where the people are kind to
me.
The people hand me sweets to make up for the bitterness
of my day.
And coins to cleanse my wardrobe of the dirt.

Then the honking of the horns ripped me out of my state.
It returned me to reality.
Ushering me back into a world with no sympathy.

The world's beauty is not what I'm running from—

It's what I'm dying for.

I press my eyes
begging for tomorrow to come.
The night insists on being a little longer
teaching me the importance of longing.
Of being patient.

Chapter VI:

Caught Like a Feather in a Jar
I am No Longer Floating

My racing heart slowing to a steady pace
at the pull of your embrace.
Your presence bringing calmness to my soul.
It is your magnetic smile
that automatically brings out mine.
It is the sound of your voice:
So clear and firm.
So toned to reassure me
that it is safe to let my guard down.
It is the sound of your constant laughter
that takes on all the weight of my tears.
It allows me to rejoice in the rare
and unburden my thoughts.

Embarking on this journey with you
feels like looking over the edge.

If I make the choice to jump over
would you be the parachute that lands me down safely?
The cushion to break my fall?
The cast placed to heal all of my broken bones?
Or would you be another prick readily waiting
to pierce a grossing scar in me infinitely?

In such a peaceful scenery…
That is where my subconscious wanders,
warning me not to let loose.
It screams: NO DON'T GET TOO CLOSE!

So that shall be my motto
The code that I love you by.
To love you just enough
That when the time comes, and you shall say goodbye.
My soul is not left with yet another broken piece
Gone with the wind.

When love introduced itself
it did so with a seducing smile
that made me aware of every hair strand.

When love introduced itself
it was with a heavy accent
that carried with it memories of my home.

When love introduced itself
we spoke of birth, death, and everything in between.
It brought laughter out of the dullest subjects.
Created a potent solution
out of the simplest ingredients:
Water. Tea. Sugar.
We shared a gaze. A touch. A kiss.
A powerful connection. An electrifying passion.

When love introduced itself
it left behind a sweet rhythm
that I hum along to when I miss him.

-    Love through Mediums

She writes of him as though honey
drools off her quill.
A flavor awakening her deepest desires.
He paints of her using the blood of his essence.
It drips from his body.
It exits out of every pore.
They are both each other's muse.
One a beast of passion.
The other a scholar of logic.
If he's the kite
then she's the string allowing him to soar within reason.
Will his passion overthrow her need to follow logic?

An age-old battle between the heart and mind...

I sat back and presented all of our moments up to the sky.
The moonlight unveiled thousands of hues I never knew,
new lenses to look through.
Underneath all those shades my thoughts became clearer.

> Love comes in many ways.
> Some loves come to teach.
> Others emerge just to leave.

In all the ruminations I realized:
It was your love that paved
off the hardened mud on my heart.
It was your love that taught me to shine past the negativity
which I thought would forever define my experiences.

You undressed my soul with your words
before you even touched me with your hands.

You showed me how my dark cave
bore resemblance to Kimberlite pipes.

With you it became a place
where rhinestones could be harvested
and glisten in my hands
with a brightness even the sun would envy.

I am sitting on the grass
pressing my body against the tree.
Begging her to take me in.
Begging her to harden my skin.

But she refuses.
She says:
"Your skin is as tough as my trunk.
It protects you just the same".

I say:
"But you're so sure of yourself.
You stand tall withstanding all that comes at you."

She says:
"There's no secret to being the strongest.
Sometimes the universe just sends things your way to cut you down.
Sometimes you get lucky but most of the time you fall."
She says:
"What's important is in the process to shake off every seed.
Spread them everywhere so they may have a chance
of withstanding more storms than you."

- Familiar stranger

It's the way you take hold of me
as if… if you let go…I might break.
Trying to conserve every piece of me.
Softly glazing my skin like an expensive piece of art
that would be ruined by your fingerprints.

A great protector ready to tend to all my wounds…
ward off all danger.
A passionate being whose love language lies in his hands
and the flick of his tongue.
As I rest in your arms
I pray that you never let go.

It's the way you embrace me…with such passion.
As though afraid to miss a second
without letting me feel your love.

Our gaze dives deep past the surface…
we see each other's souls.
A shapeless light
with no features
just radiating energy
that's familiar to us strangers.

If your world has been anything like mine
I understand why you've lost hope.
But I beg you not to give up.
Pick up your feet
start a journey towards healing.
So you can make it to me.

I hear the sounds of the tears you want to cry
and feel the breaths you hold in deep.
I pray every day that my whispers travel above all noise
to make it to your ears.
Because I swear when I am on the brink of breaking down
it is your soft whispers that carry me back up.

Take me on a trip
to the darkest corners of your mind
and I'll show you that yours is heaven compared to mine.

Tell me the things you never dared to say aloud.
Show me the things of which you are not proud.
We both have good and bad days
don't be scared, I'll never judge.
Lay out all of your cards while we play on the deck.
Grab my hand
trust that we will have a soft landing.
Hum along to the rhythms we are making.

All the things I've never said out loud
no longer remain inside.
I feel brave enough to let you hold my box of secrets.
I don't need to go searching for what we will be,
only what we are in each moment.
For that is enough for me.

I too see the blue sea.
I yearn to swim beyond its horizon.
I too desire to be crushed
by the pressure of the depth in its waters.

I too see the blue sea.
I want to be its most prized possession.

I wrote a letter to God describing all that I want in a man.
God replied by sending me you to accompany me
on this journey in accordance with his plan.

When I met you I was so eager
to share what I had held alone for so long.
The secrets that I had to carry.

After you left me all alone,
I forgot what it was like to be comfortable on my own.

As I searched for another one to share my love,
I bumped into the mirror and saw my best friend all along.

\-   Coexisting not codependent

You need to know yourself before getting to know me.
My life is not an open book to cheat your way into.
If you need to heal:
do it independently.
For I am all out from codependency.

I no longer carry the responsibility for the pain of others.
I no longer let my kindness slay me into a martyr.
I know that it's not easy to love yourself.
I had to sow a plethora of seeds.
Spend countless nights waiting and raking
to reap this love.
So I cannot credit it to you
and then risk me returning to arable land.

I can loan you advice.
You can pay me back with peace.
I have learned the best way to
help others is to lead by example.
Do not call this boundary selfish.
Because when it comes to healing me
I am the most selfless.

I've memorized all the insults that were ever thrown at me.
I've memorized all my qualities that oppose them.
I've memorized all the signs that scream toxic.
I've checked people off along with them.

My loneliness is not lonely.
It does not need any fake love to be happy.
No shallow arms to fall into.
My loneliness no longer forces me to lay with others.
With it I sleep alone and in peace.
My loneliness found comfort within me.

Cold to loss
unaffected by betrayal.
My loneliness surrounds me like a shield.
It teaches me to embrace all of my wounds
and to kiss them tenderly.

My loneliness is not lonely.
It crowns me a woman
who has become a tower of strength.
It titles me a fortified castle.

I want to use my time on earth
to just exist and experience joy fully.

I never gave consent
to be thrown in endless years
of chasing and dissatisfaction.

Annoyed at the world
for taking the little moments away from me.
For making me feel like they were not good enough.
Annoyed at myself for letting them.

Don't let the world
force you to give up your deep desires and dreams
for shallow positions
which will only leave you feeling miserable.

Don't become slaves to this materialistic world.
Live freely in yourselves.
Live freely for yourselves.

-    The Unpopular Dream

I have always imagined what it would be like to go camping.
To spark up a fire and make up horror stories.
To fall asleep amongst the stars.
To be one with the dark blue sky.

To let the wind, carry all the man-made struggles away.
To feel it lightening the weight of the cement-built walls.
To dine on hand grilled hot dogs and of course on s'mores.
To relax and enjoy steak outdoors.

To wake by the silent breath of dawn.
Where all there is to hear
are trees whispering their secrets to wildlife deer
harmonizing with morning birds.

How great would life be living in a house on wheels
accompanying the sun on its daily journey to the sea?

Has it always been in our nature
to ache for suffering?
Has it always been part of human desire
to long for drama?

If you stay silent enough
you can hear the earth
screaming at us
to ease up on it.

There was a time I wanted to be at war with silence.
Forever blasting music.
Always concealing it with my laughter.
But I have learned now to make it my home.

Growing up is funny in a way.
I used to run to my friends to make up for the lonely hours.
But now when I'm with friends I want to run to the silence.
Just to clear my brain of the chaos.

The world is dull.
It's repetitive.
It always finds a way of disappointing you.

\-   Faith over fear

What if we had more faith in each other?
What if we lessen the fear of failing each other?

I fear that all we have worked for will give birth to nothing.
I fear that Mother Nature has given up on us.
I fear that She sees us as ungrateful creatures.
I fear for the times when it will be too late to pick up
on all these warning signs She keeps throwing at us.

-    We all could use a break

We have created a systematic trap
work, eat, sleep… repeat.

Can it be okay if some days
all we do is sleep?

Chapter VII:
Final Form

I do not have to go searching far for strong women.
I do not have to even look beyond my doorsteps
to know the comfort of unconditional love
of women who did not carry me
but taught me to understand
the rhythm of their heart beats
as though I lived inside of them.

Women who bled so that I could be fed.
Women whose tears watered the plants that fan me.
women who split the oceans, crawled through the sand
on their knees and hands
to build me a path made of gold and pearls.

Women who forbade oceans to drown me.
Women who filtered gallons of salty waters
so that they flowed sweetly through me.

The strength that they carry is sometimes scary.
They move as though aware of their immortality.
Desensitized to the cuts of the world.
Stunting runways with weapons thrown deep at their backs
and heavyweights chained to their already bruised ankles.
They are warriors that slay breast cancer.

They take the hits to which I would surely crumble.
Hang their dreams up to dry.
Achieve miracles despite the obstacles.
Nothing in this world compares to You...
Kneeling for hours before God.

You will not go unappreciated.
Or
Unfamiliar to the thousand flavors
of my immeasurable gratitude.

Dear Father,

Take a moment and look at all you've accomplished.
You carried me on your shoulders ever since I could
remember.
Through the mud and tears
through the anger and hunger
you still forged a path for us to survive.

They say a father is his daughter's first love.
I am glad that you are mine.

When I look at all the sad children in the world
I wish they had a father like mine.

Little boy you are more delicate than a flower.
You deserve to be pampered.
You deserve to be watered.
You deserve space to shed your petals.

The older I get
The more apparent it becomes
how adults are still like children
looking for someone to love them.

Contrary to popular wisdom,
that need does not change with age.

On this journey
there is no deadline.
Sure, there is a point where we die.
But never before our story is meant to end.

Everything happens for a reason.
Every situation unfolds information.
Every friendship reveals transformations.
You are exactly where you are meant to be.
You are the author of your own story.

Yes, it was not your choice to begin this story.
You did not get to pick the genre
or the tools.
But you have the power to craft.
Bend the rules.
Break the box.
Scribble past the lines.
You are limitless.
Beyond measure.

- You are enough

I have no words to describe that feeling.
That one when you're standing
at the edge of your accomplishments.
You are ready to jump but there's no one to catch you.
There is no one to run that victory lap with...

But it is in your darkest days
that you see there's no one here for you.
All the people you thought
you'd be sharing this moment with...
Most of them aren't here
and it breaks your heart.

But if the right people are here
whether it be no one at all
It's a sign that you are all that you need.

I may not have the power to change the world
…but I have the power to change mine.

Forgetting is an escape.
I do not care if you call it cowardly.
Who am I to take on the knowledge of the world
and carry it like it's my duty?

Life has not been fair.
True love has been rare.
You feel lonely at times
but know that you are not alone
for God is within you.

At times, the darkness may seek to shine through
but remember you are loved.
You are blessed by the almighty above.

When your worst nightmare has come true,
what do you do?
When your world comes crashing down,
how do you not drown?
When you are surrounded by constant betrayal,
who will you trust to stay loyal?

Father God, I'm asking you to
guide me through these dark times.
To keep my faith strong
so that I may not succumb
to the chaos that surrounds me.

Help me to remember that I am loved.
Help me to never give up or lose faith
because I deserve everything great.

The worst thing in the world
is not when the one you trusted the most betrays you.
The worst thing in the world
is when you don't have God in your life.

- Self-care

We often hate to look at   the dark sides of ourselves.
We hate to reveal the sides   that are not all smiles
but made of heart   wrenching tears.
We hate to feel the mind   splitting headaches
that make you wish you   could just split yourself.

when you feel your brain   burning up from all the
thoughts   fighting at each other:
Take a breath and   split yourself open.
Use your pen.   Use your paintbrush.
Use your voice.   Use them to bleed out.
Cry until the tears are   so hot, they evaporate.
Write until your fingers   cramp.
Sing until your voice   becomes so soft
that only the wind   can carry it.

When your spirit   is aching so much
that it causes you   physical harm;
take that as a warning   to take care of yourself.

-    Growth

Rudy Francisco once said:
"The difference between a garden and a graveyard is what you choose to bury in the ground."

That is why
I choose to engrave positive thoughts in my mind
and turn my words into bees.
Spreading positivity like pollen.
Hoping to leave a trail of gardens
in the minds of those around me.

Because you see...
the freedom
in this space
has always been a little complicated.
A little restricted.
A little suffocated by negative thoughts.
When I prayed for clarity only rainstorms blew my way.

But I've come to understand
that it takes the cruelest of weather
to clear the land of debris.
To make way for gardens to grow.

Society has made it a habit
of staying attached to our trauma.
Whether it be from childhood,
from relationships or from friendships.
We use them as scapegoats to excuse our unhealthy habits.

We forget that letting them go
is as important
as recognizing them.

There is no changing what happened.
Focus on the now. Be in the moment.
Do not let these thoughts paralyze you.
Do not let them keep you stuck in the same routine.

Stop making the past the focus of your present.
Start thinking about where you are going from there.
Start envisioning what fruit you are about to reap
from the seeds you are planting.

When fall comes
your leaves start to shed.
Do not be scared.
You are only losing your old self.
The one made up of unprocessed trauma.

Lean into the wind.
Soon you will see
how beautiful growth can be.
Your spring will come.
Your garden will grow.

This book started with love, and it ends in hope.
A reminder to hold on to both.

ACKNOWLEDGMENTS

I would like to express my gratitude to everyone who helped make this book possible. Every day, I am surrounded by talented, beautiful, and driven people who inspire me. Everyone in my life has contributed to this book whether by giving me a word of motivation, inspiration, or by pushing me to be my creative self. To my mother and father, as well as friends, and other family members. Angel Nduka-Nwosu, my editor. Janni Pillerva, my talented illustrator. To the best of us all, my wonderful God.

Instagram- @ruminativewords

Facebook- @fritzinielavoile

Twitter- @ruminativewords

ABOUT THE AUTHOR

Fritzinie Lavoile is a Haitian poet and author who recently released Ruminative Words, her first poetry collection. Her enthusiasm for reading quotes evolved into a passion for wordplay and creativity. Poetry allows her to express her vulnerability while also taking ownership of the difficulties she has overcome. She aspires to help others become better versions of themselves by sharing the lessons she has learned. Writing poetry has always been her safety net, catching her when she is at her lowest or at her highest. She hopes that this book has helped you find a safe space within yourself. And inspired you to become your own safety net